GOODSON MUMBA

The Performance Paradigm
Building a Culture of Excellence

Copyright © 2024 by Goodson Mumba

All rights reserved. No part of this publication may be reproduced, stored or transmitted in any form or by any means, electronic, mechanical, photocopying, recording, scanning, or otherwise without written permission from the publisher. It is illegal to copy this book, post it to a website, or distribute it by any other means without permission.

First edition

ISBN: 9798334770584

This book was professionally typeset on Reedsy. Find out more at reedsy.com

Contents

Preface — v
Acknowledgement — vii
Dedication — viii
Disclaimer — ix

1. Chapter One: Introduction to a Crisis — 1
2. Chapter Two: Setting Performance Management Objectives — 8
3. Chapter Three: Performance Metrics and Key Performance... — 14
4. Chapter Four: Performance Feedback and Evaluation — 20
5. Chapter Five: Performance Appraisal Systems — 26
6. Chapter Six: Performance Recognition and Rewards — 33
7. Chapter Seven: Training and Development for Performance... — 39
8. Chapter Eight: Technology in Performance Management — 45
9. Chapter Nine: Performance Management for Remote and... — 51
10. Chapter Ten: Performance Management for Different... — 58
11. Chapter Eleven: Legal and Ethical considerations in... — 64

12	Chapter Twelve: Continuous Improvement of Performance...	69
13	Chapter Thirteen: Case Studies in Effective Performance...	75
14	Chapter Fourteen: Future Trends in Performance Management	80
15	Chapter Fifteen: Conclusion and Implementation Strategies	86
About the Author		92

Preface

In today's dynamic and competitive landscape, organizations face a relentless pursuit: achieving excellence. This pursuit is not merely a goal but a continuous journey—a journey shaped by the collective efforts of individuals, guided by a shared vision, and fueled by a commitment to relentless improvement.

"The Performance Paradigm: Building a Culture of Excellence" delves into the essence of what makes organizations thrive in the face of challenges and uncertainties. It explores the pivotal role of culture in shaping performance, emphasizing that true excellence transcends mere skill—it resides in the very fabric of how an organization operates, thinks, and grows.

Through years of research, and insightful case studies, this book offers a comprehensive framework for cultivating a culture that champions excellence. It examines the interplay between leadership, strategy, and execution, illustrating how each component contributes to a cohesive and high-performing organizational ecosystem.

At its core, this book challenges conventional thinking and invites leaders and practitioners alike to rethink their approaches to achieving excellence. It advocates for a paradigm shift—a shift from seeing performance as a series of isolated achievements to embracing it as a collective ethos ingrained in every facet of organizational life.

Drawing on a blend of academic rigor and practical wisdom,

"The Performance Paradigm" equips readers with actionable strategies to foster a culture where excellence becomes not just a goal, but a natural way of being. It empowers leaders to inspire, teams to collaborate, and individuals to unleash their full potential in service of a shared purpose.

As you embark on this exploration of excellence, may this book serve as a guiding light—a beacon illuminating pathways to sustained success and fulfillment in the pursuit of organizational greatness.

Welcome to "The Performance Paradigm: Building a Culture of Excellence."

Goodson Mumba

Acknowledgement

I would like to eternally and gratefully acknowledge the Almighty God for the infinite intelligence from His universal mind where we draw from all that we come to know and are yet to know. May I also acknowledge and thank everyone that has played a part in my journey of life in terms of spiritual, moral, emotional and material support.

Dedication

I extend my sincerest gratitude to my beloved wife, Edith Mumba, and our children, Angelina, Lubuto, Letticia, Lulumbi, and Butusho, for their unwavering support and understanding throughout the conception, writing, and eventual publication of this book, despite the sacrifices and challenges they endured.

Disclaimer

This book is a work of fiction. Names, characters, businesses, places, events, and incidents are either the products of the author's imagination or used in a fictitious manner. Any resemblance to actual persons, living or dead, or actual events is purely coincidental.

1

Chapter One: Introduction to a Crisis

In the bustling corporate headquarters of BrightTech Inc., Emma, the seasoned HR manager, sat in her office, surrounded by stacks of papers and a looming sense of urgency. The CEO's message earlier that day echoed in her mind like a warning bell: "Our performance management system is failing us, Emma. Employee morale is plummeting, and our productivity is stagnant. We need a solution, and we need it fast."

Emma felt the weight of the challenge ahead of her as she glanced at the clock ticking away on her desk. With each passing minute, the pressure mounted. She knew she had to act swiftly and decisively.

Gathering her courage, Emma stepped into the executive boardroom, where the leadership team awaited her presentation. As she began to outline the shortcomings of the current performance management system, she was met with skeptical glances and furrowed brows. Some executives seemed reluctant to acknowledge the severity of the situation, clinging to the familiarity of the status quo.

But Emma refused to be deterred by their resistance. With unwavering determination, she painted a vivid picture of the consequences of inaction – decreased employee engagement, talent attrition, and ultimately, diminished organizational success. She emphasized the critical role that a robust performance management system played in fostering a culture of excellence and driving business outcomes.

Guided by the principles outlined in her trusted companion, "Designing a Performance Management System: Strategies for Optimizing Organizational Success and Employee Performance," Emma challenged the leadership team to embrace change and embark on a journey of transformation. She stressed the need for a dynamic and employee-centric approach to performance management, one that would empower individuals to thrive and contribute to the company's overarching goals.

As the meeting drew to a close, Emma could sense a shift in the room. Despite the initial skepticism, a flicker of hope ignited in the eyes of some executives. The seeds of change had been planted, and Emma was determined to nurture them into fruition.

Leaving the boardroom with a renewed sense of purpose, Emma knew that the road ahead would be fraught with challenges. But she was ready to face them head-on, armed with her expertise, determination, and the invaluable insights gleaned from her trusted companion.

With a sense of determination fueling her every step, Emma knew that the first hurdle she needed to overcome was convincing the skeptical executives of the critical importance of performance management. As she continued her presentation, she delved deeper into the fundamental principles underlying effective performance management, each word imbued with passion and conviction.

"Performance management isn't just about ticking boxes or filling out forms," Emma declared, her voice ringing with sincerity. "It's about empowering our employees to reach their full potential, driving organizational success, and fostering a culture of excellence."

She illustrated her point with vivid examples of companies that had flourished under the guidance of robust performance management systems, their stories serving as beacons of inspiration amidst the sea of doubt. From startups to industry titans, the common thread that wove through their success stories was a commitment to nurturing talent, providing constructive feedback, and aligning individual efforts with overarching organizational goals.

But Emma didn't stop there. Drawing from her own experiences and the insights gleaned from her trusty companion, she painted a compelling picture of the myriad benefits that a well-designed performance management system could bring to BrightTech. Increased employee engagement, enhanced productivity, talent retention – the possibilities were limitless.

As Emma spoke, she could sense a shift in the atmosphere of the room. The skepticism that had once hung thick in the air began to dissipate, replaced by a growing sense of curiosity and receptivity. The executives leaned in, their interest piqued by Emma's impassioned plea for change.

By the time Emma concluded her presentation, she could see a glimmer of understanding dawning in the eyes of the executives. They may not have been fully convinced yet, but they were starting to grasp the transformative potential of a revamped performance management system.

With the first step taken, Emma knew that the journey ahead would be long and arduous. But as she looked around the room at the faces of her colleagues, she felt a surge of optimism coursing through her veins. The seeds of change had been planted, and with perseverance and determination, they would surely take root and flourish.

As Emma delved into the historical context and evolution of performance management systems, she transported the executives on a journey through time, tracing the origins of modern performance management practices back to their roots.

"Within the annals of corporate history lies a rich tapestry of performance management evolution," Emma began, her voice taking on a melodious cadence as she spoke. "From the early days of scientific management pioneered by Frederick Taylor to the emergence of behavioral management theories championed by luminaries such as Douglas McGregor, the landscape of performance management has undergone a series of transformations, each one leaving an indelible mark on the practices we see today."

With each passing decade, Emma painted a vivid picture of the shifting paradigms that had shaped the evolution of performance management – from the rigid hierarchies of the industrial age to the rise of knowledge-based economies and the dawn of the digital era.

She recounted stories of visionary leaders who had dared to challenge the status quo, ushering in new methodologies and frameworks that sought to harness the full potential of human capital. From Peter Drucker's seminal work on management by objectives to the pioneering efforts of early adopters of 360-degree feedback, Emma showcased the ingenuity and innovation that had propelled performance management into the modern era.

But as she spoke, Emma also highlighted the pitfalls and shortcomings that had plagued performance management throughout its history – the tendency towards bureaucratic rigidity, the overemphasis on numerical targets at the expense of holistic evaluation, and the perpetuation of bias and inequality in performance appraisal processes.

With each revelation, Emma's words resonated with the executives, prompting them to reflect on their own experiences and perceptions of performance management. The stories of triumph and tribulation painted a nuanced picture of an ever-evolving discipline, one that was both shaped by its past and poised to embrace the challenges of the future.

As Emma concluded her exploration of performance management's historical landscape, she left the executives with a sense of awe and wonder at the journey they had embarked upon. The lessons of the past served as guiding beacons, illuminating the path forward as they prepared to chart a new course for BrightTech's performance management future.

As Emma delved into the common challenges faced in performance management, she could sense the tension in the room thickening. The executives, once captivated by her narrative, now sat with furrowed brows and crossed arms, their skepticism palpable in the air.

"Performance management is not without its hurdles," Emma began, her voice steady despite the growing unease in the room. "From ineffective communication channels to biases in evaluation processes, there are myriad obstacles that organizations must navigate in their quest for excellence."

With each challenge she outlined, Emma painted a vivid picture of the struggles that organizations faced in their attempts to implement and maintain effective performance management systems. The executives nodded in recognition as she spoke of the difficulties in setting clear and meaningful performance objectives, the pitfalls of relying solely on quantitative metrics, and the pervasive fear of feedback that stifled growth and innovation.

But Emma didn't stop there. With unwavering resolve, she tackled head-on the more contentious issues that had long plagued performance management discourse – the specter of bias and discrimination that lurked within appraisal processes, the lack of transparency and accountability in performance evaluations, and the disconnect between individual goals and organizational objectives.

As she spoke, Emma could see the executives' expressions shifting from skepticism to contemplation. The challenges she outlined resonated with their own experiences and observations, sparking a glimmer of recognition and understanding in their eyes.

But Emma wasn't content to leave it at that. With a renewed sense of purpose, she offered solutions and strategies for overcoming these challenges, drawing from her own experiences and the insights gleaned from her trusty companion.

"By fostering a culture of open communication, providing regular and constructive feedback, and ensuring transparency and fairness in our evaluation processes, we can overcome these challenges and unlock the full potential of our workforce," Emma declared, her voice ringing with conviction.

As she concluded her exploration of the common challenges faced in performance management, Emma could sense a shift in the atmosphere of the room. The skepticism that had once hung heavy in the air had been replaced by a newfound sense of determination and resolve.

2

Chapter Two: Setting Performance Management Objectives

In the heart of BrightTech's corporate headquarters, Emma stood before a gathering of department heads and managers, her eyes ablaze with determination. The task at hand was daunting, but Emma was undeterred. With the CEO's mandate echoing in her mind, she embarked on the next phase of her mission: setting performance management objectives that would chart the course for organizational success.

"Setting performance management objectives is the cornerstone of our journey towards excellence," Emma declared, her voice ringing out with authority. "It's not just about ticking boxes or meeting quotas – it's about aligning individual aspirations with organizational goals, empowering our employees to reach their full potential, and driving collective success."

As she spoke, Emma could feel the energy in the room shift, her words igniting a spark of inspiration in the hearts of her audience. Gone were the skeptical glances and furrowed brows; in their place were nods of agreement and eager anticipation.

Drawing from the principles outlined in her trusty com-

CHAPTER TWO: SETTING PERFORMANCE MANAGEMENT OBJECTIVES

panion, Emma guided her audience through the intricacies of setting performance objectives that were SMART – Specific, Measurable, Achievable, Relevant, and Time-bound. She emphasized the importance of clarity and specificity, urging her colleagues to articulate objectives that were both meaningful and attainable.

But Emma didn't stop there. With characteristic thoroughness, she delved into the nuances of aligning individual goals with overarching organizational objectives, illustrating her points with real-world examples and case studies that brought her message to life.

"By aligning our individual objectives with the broader vision and mission of BrightTech, we can harness the collective power of our workforce and propel our organization to new heights of success," Emma proclaimed, her voice resonating with passion and conviction.

As the meeting drew to a close, Emma could sense a palpable shift in the atmosphere of the room. The executives and managers who had once been skeptical of change now stood united in their commitment to the journey ahead. The seeds of transformation had been planted, and Emma knew that with determination and perseverance, they would surely blossom into fruition.

With the momentum of her impassioned speech still lingering in the air, Emma turned her attention to the critical task of defining organizational goals and objectives. It was a pivotal moment in BrightTech's journey towards excellence, and Emma knew that the stakes had never been higher.

"Organizational goals are the guiding stars that steer our ship towards success," Emma declared, her voice ringing out with authority. "They provide us with a clear direction and a sense of purpose, guiding our actions and decisions as we navigate the turbulent waters of the corporate world."

As she spoke, Emma could feel the energy in the room crackling with anticipation, her words igniting a spark of inspiration in the hearts of her audience. Gone were the doubts and skepticism of moments past; in their place was a sense of purpose and determination that permeated the very air.

Drawing from the principles outlined in her trusty companion, Emma guided her audience through the process of defining organizational goals that were ambitious yet achievable, visionary yet grounded in reality. She emphasized the importance of alignment – ensuring that each goal served as a building block in the edifice of BrightTech's overarching vision and mission.

But Emma didn't stop there. With characteristic thoroughness, she delved into the nuances of translating these lofty aspirations into concrete, actionable objectives that could be pursued with vigor and determination. She urged her colleagues to think strategically, to break down complex goals into manageable tasks, and to prioritize ruthlessly in pursuit of success.

"By defining clear and compelling organizational goals, we lay the foundation for a future filled with possibility and promise," Emma proclaimed, her voice ringing with conviction. "Together, we can chart a course towards greatness, one step at a time."

As the meeting drew to a close, Emma could sense a palpable shift in the atmosphere of the room. The executives and managers who had once been daunted by the challenges ahead now stood united in their commitment to the journey. The seeds of transformation had been planted, and Emma knew that with diligence and determination, they would surely blossom

CHAPTER TWO: SETTING PERFORMANCE MANAGEMENT OBJECTIVES

into fruition.

With the foundation of organizational goals firmly established, Emma turned her attention to the critical task of aligning individual and team objectives with BrightTech's overarching vision. It was a pivotal moment in their journey towards excellence, and Emma knew that the success of their performance management system hinged upon this crucial step.

"Aligning individual and team objectives with our organizational goals is the key to unlocking our collective potential," Emma declared, her voice resonating with authority. "It's not enough to simply set lofty aspirations – we must ensure that each member of our team understands their role in achieving these objectives and is empowered to contribute their unique talents and skills."

As she spoke, Emma could feel the energy in the room shifting, her words igniting a spark of inspiration in the hearts of her audience. Gone were the doubts and uncertainties of moments past; in their place was a sense of purpose and determination that permeated the very air.

Drawing from the principles outlined in her trusty companion, Emma guided her audience through the process of aligning individual and team objectives with organizational goals. She emphasized the importance of clarity and transparency, urging her colleagues to communicate clearly and consistently with their teams, ensuring that everyone understood the role they played in the bigger picture.

But Emma didn't stop there. With characteristic thoroughness, she delved into the nuances of cascading goals down through the organization, ensuring that each level of the hierarchy was aligned and focused on achieving the same overarching objectives. She encouraged her colleagues to foster a culture of collaboration and accountability, where individuals felt empowered to support one another in pursuit of shared goals.

"By aligning our individual and team objectives with the broader vision of BrightTech, we can harness the collective power of our workforce and propel our organization to new heights of success," Emma proclaimed, her voice ringing with conviction.

As the meeting drew to a close, Emma could sense a palpable shift in the atmosphere of the room. The executives and managers who had once been daunted by the challenges ahead now stood united in their commitment to the journey. The seeds of transformation had been planted, and Emma knew that with diligence and determination, they would surely blossom into fruition.

With the resonance of her previous words still lingering in the air, Emma shifted her focus to the critical task of setting performance objectives using the SMART criteria. It was a pivotal moment in BrightTech's journey towards excellence, and Emma knew that the success of their performance management system hinged upon the clarity and specificity of these objectives.

"The SMART criteria provide us with a roadmap for setting objectives that are clear, actionable, and aligned with our organizational goals," Emma declared, her voice ringing out with authority. "By adhering to these principles, we can ensure that our efforts are focused and our progress measurable."

As she spoke, Emma could feel the energy in the room crackling with anticipation, her words igniting a spark of inspiration in the hearts of her audience. Gone were the doubts and uncertainties of moments past; in their place was a sense

CHAPTER TWO: SETTING PERFORMANCE MANAGEMENT OBJECTIVES

of purpose and determination that permeated the very air.

Drawing from the principles outlined in her trusty companion, Emma guided her audience through the components of the SMART criteria – Specific, Measurable, Achievable, Relevant, and Time-bound. She emphasized the importance of clarity and specificity, urging her colleagues to articulate objectives that were both meaningful and attainable.

But Emma didn't stop there. With characteristic thoroughness, she delved into the nuances of each component, illustrating her points with real-world examples and case studies that brought her message to life. She encouraged her colleagues to think critically about their objectives, to break them down into actionable tasks, and to set realistic deadlines for achievement.

"By adhering to the SMART criteria, we can ensure that our objectives are not just lofty aspirations, but concrete action plans that propel us towards success," Emma proclaimed, her voice ringing with conviction.

As the meeting drew to a close, Emma could sense a palpable shift in the atmosphere of the room. The executives and managers who had once been daunted by the challenges ahead now stood united in their commitment to the journey. The seeds of transformation had been planted, and Emma knew that with diligence and determination, they would surely blossom into fruition.

3

Chapter Three: Performance Metrics and Key Performance Indicators (KPIs)

As the sun dipped below the horizon, casting long shadows across the gleaming towers of BrightTech's corporate headquarters, Emma gathered her team for a pivotal meeting. The task at hand was daunting, but Emma was undeterred. With the CEO's mandate echoing in her mind, she embarked on the next phase of her mission: defining performance metrics and Key Performance Indicators (KPIs) that would drive organizational success.

"Performance metrics and KPIs are the compass by which we navigate our journey towards excellence," Emma declared, her voice ringing out with authority. "They provide us with valuable insights into our progress, guiding our actions and decisions as we strive to achieve our goals."

As she spoke, Emma could feel the energy in the room crackling with anticipation, her words igniting a spark of inspiration in the hearts of her team. Gone were the doubts and uncertainties of moments past; in their place was a sense of purpose and determination that permeated the very air.

CHAPTER THREE: PERFORMANCE METRICS AND KEY PERFORMANCE...

Drawing from the principles outlined in her trusty companion, Emma guided her team through the intricacies of defining performance metrics and KPIs that were relevant, actionable, and aligned with BrightTech's overarching objectives. She emphasized the importance of clarity and specificity, urging her colleagues to select metrics that provided meaningful insights into their progress towards key goals.

But Emma didn't stop there. With characteristic thoroughness, she delved into the nuances of each metric, illustrating her points with real-world examples and case studies that brought her message to life. She encouraged her team to think critically about the metrics they selected, to ensure that they captured the full spectrum of performance and provided a comprehensive view of organizational health.

"By defining performance metrics and KPIs that are aligned with our strategic objectives, we can measure our progress with precision and clarity," Emma proclaimed, her voice ringing with conviction.

As the meeting drew to a close, Emma could sense a palpable shift in the atmosphere of the room. The members of her team who had once been daunted by the challenges ahead now stood united in their commitment to the journey. The seeds of transformation had been planted, and Emma knew that with diligence and determination, they would surely blossom into fruition.

As the city lights flickered to life outside the towering windows of BrightTech's boardroom, Emma and her team delved deeper into the task of identifying relevant performance metrics. It was a pivotal moment in their journey towards excellence, and Emma knew that the success of their performance management system hinged upon the selection of metrics that truly captured the essence of organizational success.

"Relevant performance metrics are the lifeblood of our performance management system," Emma declared, her voice resonating with authority. "They provide us with valuable insights into our progress towards our goals, enabling us to make informed decisions and course corrections along the way."

As she spoke, Emma could feel the energy in the room crackling with anticipation, her words igniting a spark of inspiration in the hearts of her team. Gone were the doubts and uncertainties of moments past; in their place was a sense of purpose and determination that permeated the very air.

Drawing from the principles outlined in her trusty companion, Emma guided her team through the process of identifying performance metrics that were relevant, actionable, and aligned with BrightTech's strategic objectives. She emphasized the importance of selecting metrics that provided a comprehensive view of organizational performance, capturing both quantitative and qualitative aspects of success.

But Emma didn't stop there. With characteristic thoroughness, she delved into the nuances of each metric, illustrating her points with real-world examples and case studies that brought her message to life. She encouraged her team to think critically about the metrics they selected, to ensure that they reflected the unique challenges and opportunities facing BrightTech in the ever-evolving landscape of the corporate world.

"By identifying relevant performance metrics, we can ensure that our performance management system is not just a collection of data points, but a powerful tool for driving organizational success," Emma proclaimed, her voice ringing with conviction.

As the meeting drew to a close, Emma could sense a palpable

shift in the atmosphere of the room. The members of her team who had once been daunted by the challenges ahead now stood united in their commitment to the journey. The seeds of transformation had been planted, and Emma knew that with diligence and determination, they would surely blossom into fruition.

As the moon cast its gentle glow over the city skyline, Emma and her team delved deeper into the task of establishing meaningful Key Performance Indicators (KPIs) for different roles and departments within BrightTech. It was a crucial step in their journey towards excellence, and Emma knew that the success of their performance management system relied on the ability to tailor KPIs to the unique needs and objectives of each team.

"Meaningful KPIs are the compass that guides each member of our organization towards success," Emma declared, her voice carrying the weight of conviction. "They provide us with clarity and direction, enabling us to focus our efforts on the activities that matter most."

As she spoke, Emma could sense the anticipation in the room, her words resonating with each member of her team. Gone were the doubts and hesitations of earlier discussions; in their place was a sense of purpose and determination that filled the room with energy.

Drawing from the principles outlined in her trusty companion, Emma guided her team through the process of identifying KPIs that were relevant, actionable, and aligned with the goals of each department. She emphasized the importance of collaboration and communication, urging her colleagues to work together to ensure that KPIs were meaningful and impactful.

But Emma didn't stop there. With her characteristic attention to detail, she delved into the nuances of each department, taking into account the unique challenges and opportunities they faced. From sales to marketing, from operations to finance, Emma worked tirelessly to ensure that each team had KPIs that were tailored to their specific needs.

"By establishing meaningful KPIs for each role and department, we empower our teams to excel in their areas of expertise," Emma proclaimed, her voice filled with confidence.

As the meeting drew to a close, Emma could feel a sense of accomplishment wash over her team. The once-daunting task of establishing KPIs had been transformed into a collaborative effort, with each member contributing their expertise and insights to the process.

As the night deepened, casting shadows across the conference room, Emma and her team delved into the delicate task of balancing quantitative and qualitative measures within BrightTech's performance management system. It was a pivotal moment in their journey towards excellence, and Emma knew that the success of their system relied on striking the right balance between hard numbers and nuanced insights.

"Quantitative measures provide us with valuable data points, but it is the qualitative measures that give us a deeper understanding of our organization's health and performance," Emma declared, her voice steady with determination. "By balancing both, we can ensure that our performance management system is comprehensive and meaningful."

As she spoke, Emma could feel the tension in the room, her words stirring something deep within each member of her team. Gone were the hesitations and uncertainties of earlier discussions; in their place was a sense of clarity and purpose that filled the room with a quiet intensity.

Drawing from the principles outlined in her trusty companion, Emma guided her team through the process of identifying both quantitative and qualitative measures that were relevant and impactful. She emphasized the importance of looking beyond the numbers, urging her colleagues to consider factors such as employee satisfaction, innovation, and organizational culture.

But Emma didn't stop there. With her characteristic attention to detail, she delved into the nuances of each measure, exploring the ways in which quantitative data could be complemented by qualitative insights to provide a more holistic view of performance.

"By balancing quantitative and qualitative measures, we can gain a deeper understanding of our organization's strengths and weaknesses, enabling us to make more informed decisions and drive meaningful change," Emma proclaimed, her voice resonating with conviction.

As the meeting drew to a close, Emma could feel a sense of satisfaction wash over her team. The once-daunting task of balancing quantitative and qualitative measures had been transformed into a collaborative effort, with each member contributing their expertise and insights to the process.

4

Chapter Four: Performance Feedback and Evaluation

As the sun rose over the horizon, casting a warm glow across the sleek offices of BrightTech, Emma gathered her team for a crucial discussion on performance feedback and evaluation. It was a pivotal chapter in their journey towards building a culture of excellence, and Emma knew that effective feedback was the cornerstone of a successful performance management system.

"Performance feedback is not just about evaluating past performance; it's about guiding future growth and development," Emma declared, her voice resonating with authority. "By providing timely and constructive feedback, we empower our employees to reach their full potential and drive organizational success."

As she spoke, Emma could feel the energy in the room shift, her words igniting a spark of inspiration in the hearts of her team. Gone were the doubts and uncertainties of moments past; in their place was a sense of purpose and determination that permeated the very air.

CHAPTER FOUR: PERFORMANCE FEEDBACK AND EVALUATION

Drawing from the principles outlined in her trusty companion, Emma guided her team through the process of establishing a feedback culture rooted in transparency, openness, and mutual respect. She emphasized the importance of regular check-ins and one-on-one discussions, urging her colleagues to provide feedback that was specific, actionable, and focused on growth.

But Emma didn't stop there. With her characteristic empathy, she delved into the nuances of giving and receiving feedback, exploring the delicate balance between constructive criticism and praise. She encouraged her team to approach feedback conversations with empathy and compassion, recognizing the unique strengths and challenges of each individual.

"Effective feedback is a gift that has the power to transform performance and drive organizational success," Emma proclaimed, her voice filled with conviction.

As the meeting drew to a close, Emma could sense a palpable shift in the atmosphere of the room. The once-daunting task of providing feedback had been transformed into an opportunity for growth and development, with each member of her team committed to supporting one another on their journey towards excellence.

As the morning sun streamed through the windows of the conference room, casting a warm glow over the polished table, Emma shifted her focus to the critical aspect of providing timely and constructive feedback. It was a moment of truth in their journey towards building a culture of excellence, and Emma knew that the effectiveness of their performance management system hinged on this key component.

"Feedback is not a one-time event; it's an ongoing dialogue that fosters growth and development," Emma began, her voice carrying the weight of experience. "By providing timely and constructive feedback, we empower our employees to course-correct and strive for excellence."

As she spoke, Emma could feel the energy in the room shift once again, her words igniting a sense of purpose and determination in her team. Gone were the hesitations and uncertainties of earlier discussions; in their place was a renewed commitment to driving organizational success through meaningful feedback.

Drawing from the principles outlined in her trusty companion, Emma guided her team through the process of delivering feedback that was both timely and constructive. She emphasized the importance of specificity and clarity, urging her colleagues to focus on behaviors and outcomes rather than personal traits.

But Emma didn't stop there. With her characteristic empathy, she delved into the nuances of feedback delivery, exploring the delicate balance between honesty and kindness. She encouraged her team to approach feedback conversations with empathy and compassion, recognizing the impact their words could have on their colleagues' morale and motivation.

"Timely and constructive feedback is a gift that has the power to transform performance and drive organizational success," Emma declared, her voice ringing with conviction.

As the meeting drew to a close, Emma could sense a palpable shift in the atmosphere of the room. The once-daunting task of providing feedback had been transformed into an opportunity for growth and development, with each member of her team committed to supporting one another on their journey towards excellence.

As the afternoon sun cast long shadows across the office floor, Emma gathered her team once again to tackle the next

CHAPTER FOUR: PERFORMANCE FEEDBACK AND EVALUATION

crucial aspect of their performance management overhaul: conducting fair and unbiased performance evaluations. It was a topic fraught with challenges and complexities, but Emma approached it with the same determination and resolve that had guided her thus far.

"Ensuring fairness and objectivity in our performance evaluations is paramount," Emma began, her voice steady and resolute. "We must strive to create a system that recognizes and rewards merit, regardless of personal biases or preconceptions."

As she spoke, Emma could sense the weight of responsibility settling over the room. The task ahead was daunting, but Emma knew that with diligence and vigilance, they could overcome any obstacles in their path.

Drawing from the principles outlined in her trusty companion, Emma guided her team through the process of conducting fair and unbiased performance evaluations. She emphasized the importance of setting clear evaluation criteria and standards, ensuring that all employees were held to the same objective benchmarks.

But Emma didn't stop there. With her characteristic empathy and insight, she delved into the intricacies of mitigating unconscious biases in the evaluation process. She encouraged her team to approach evaluations with an open mind and a willingness to challenge their own assumptions, recognizing that unchecked biases could undermine the integrity of their assessments.

"Fairness and objectivity are not just ideals to strive for; they are essential principles that underpin the credibility of our performance management system," Emma declared, her voice ringing with conviction.

As the meeting drew to a close, Emma could sense a renewed

sense of purpose and determination among her team. The road ahead would be challenging, but they were united in their commitment to building a culture of excellence based on fairness, transparency, and integrity.

As the sun dipped below the horizon, casting a warm glow over the office, Emma gathered her team once more to tackle the critical aspect of addressing performance issues and offering support for improvement. It was a task that required empathy, tact, and a genuine commitment to the well-being and growth of each employee.

"Addressing performance issues is not about pointing fingers or assigning blame," Emma began, her voice measured yet compassionate. "It's about recognizing that every employee has the potential for growth and improvement, and it's our responsibility to support them on that journey."

With the principles outlined in her trusted companion guiding her, Emma led her team through the delicate process of identifying and addressing performance issues with sensitivity and respect. She stressed the importance of providing constructive feedback in a timely manner, offering specific examples and actionable suggestions for improvement.

But Emma knew that addressing performance issues was only half the battle. Equally important was offering the necessary support and resources to help employees succeed. Whether it was additional training, mentorship opportunities, or simply a listening ear, Emma encouraged her team to go above and beyond to ensure that every employee had the tools they needed to thrive.

"As leaders, it's our duty to nurture and support our employees, even when they're facing challenges," Emma affirmed, her words resonating with conviction.

As the meeting drew to a close, Emma could sense a palpable shift in the room. Where there had once been apprehension and uncertainty, there was now a shared sense of purpose and determination. Together, they would not only address performance issues but also cultivate a culture of support, growth, and resilience.

5

Chapter Five: Performance Appraisal Systems

In the heart of the corporate headquarters, Emma convened a meeting of key stakeholders to unveil the new performance appraisal system, a cornerstone of the revitalized performance management framework. As she stood before the assembled team, Emma could feel the weight of anticipation in the air.

"Today marks a significant milestone in our journey toward building a culture of excellence," Emma declared, her voice filled with conviction. "Our new performance appraisal system is not just a tool for evaluation, but a catalyst for growth, development, and success."

With the principles of fairness, transparency, and employee-centricity guiding her, Emma outlined the key features of the new appraisal system. Gone were the days of rigid, once-a-year evaluations; instead, the new system embraced a continuous feedback model, providing employees with regular opportunities to receive and provide feedback on their performance.

"But perhaps the most transformative aspect of our new

appraisal system is its focus on development," Emma continued. "Rather than viewing appraisals as a mere formality, we see them as an opportunity for meaningful dialogue, goal-setting, and skill enhancement."

As Emma elaborated on the various components of the appraisal system—goal setting, competency assessment, performance feedback—the room buzzed with excitement and anticipation. It was clear that her vision for a performance management system that empowered and inspired employees had struck a chord with her colleagues.

But Emma knew that implementing the new appraisal system would not be without its challenges. From resistance to change to logistical hurdles, there would be obstacles to overcome. Yet, armed with determination, creativity, and the unwavering support of her team, Emma was confident that they would navigate these challenges together.

"As we embark on this next phase of our journey, let us remember that our ultimate goal is not just to improve performance, but to cultivate a culture where every employee can thrive and succeed," Emma concluded, her words echoing through the room.

As the meeting adjourned and the team dispersed to begin the implementation process, Emma felt a sense of pride and anticipation. The journey ahead would be challenging, but she knew that together, they would continue to push the boundaries of what was possible and build a culture of excellence that would define BrightTech for years to come.

As Emma delved deeper into the redesign of the performance appraisal system, she recognized the need to explore various types of performance appraisal methods to ensure they selected the most effective approach for BrightTech. With her team by her side, she embarked on a journey to explore different methodologies, each offering unique insights into employee performance.

The conference room buzzed with anticipation as Emma introduced the concept of 360-degree feedback—a comprehensive approach that involved gathering feedback from multiple sources, including peers, subordinates, supervisors, and even clients. As she explained the benefits of this holistic approach to performance appraisal, she could see the intrigue in her colleagues' eyes.

"Incorporating 360-degree feedback allows us to gain a more comprehensive understanding of an employee's strengths, weaknesses, and areas for improvement," Emma explained, her voice filled with enthusiasm. "By soliciting input from various perspectives, we can provide employees with a well-rounded assessment of their performance."

Next, Emma turned her attention to graphic rating scales—a more traditional approach that involved evaluating employees based on predefined criteria and rating scales. While not as comprehensive as 360-degree feedback, graphic rating scales offered simplicity and ease of use, making them a valuable tool for performance appraisal.

"As we consider the different types of performance appraisal methods, it's important to strike a balance between comprehensiveness and practicality," Emma emphasized. "Each method has its strengths and limitations, and it's up to us to choose the approach that best aligns with our organizational goals and values."

As the discussion unfolded, Emma and her team weighed the pros and cons of each method, considering factors such as scalability, reliability, and employee acceptance. It was a complex decision, but one that would ultimately shape the future of performance management at BrightTech.

In the end, Emma knew that whatever method they chose, it would be grounded in the principles of fairness, transparency, and employee empowerment—the cornerstones of the new performance management paradigm they were building together. With their collective expertise and dedication, Emma was confident that they would design a performance appraisal system that not only evaluated performance but also inspired growth, development, and excellence among BrightTech's employees.

With the foundation of performance appraisal methods laid out, Emma turned her attention to the design and implementation of performance appraisal forms—a critical component of the new performance management system at BrightTech. As she gathered her team in the conference room once again, she could feel the energy and determination palpable in the air.

"We need performance appraisal forms that are not only user-friendly but also aligned with our organizational goals and values," Emma stated firmly, setting the tone for the discussion.

Together, they brainstormed ideas, drawing on their collective expertise and insights to craft appraisal forms that would facilitate fair and constructive evaluations. Emma emphasized the importance of incorporating both quantitative and qualitative measures, ensuring a comprehensive assessment of employee performance.

"We want our employees to feel empowered and supported throughout the appraisal process," Emma explained. "These forms should serve as a tool for growth and development, not just a means of evaluation."

As they worked through the details, Emma and her team

considered various elements to include in the appraisal forms—goal attainment, core competencies, professional development goals, and areas for improvement, among others. They also discussed the importance of providing space for comments and feedback, encouraging open and honest communication between employees and their evaluators.

"It's crucial that our forms reflect our commitment to transparency and fairness," Emma emphasized. "Employees should feel confident that their performance is being evaluated objectively and that they have a voice in the process."

With each detail carefully considered and refined, the team finalized the design of the performance appraisal forms, ready to move forward with implementation. Emma felt a sense of pride and excitement as she looked around the room, knowing that they were one step closer to realizing their vision of a performance management system that truly fostered excellence and innovation at BrightTech.

As they prepared to roll out the new forms, Emma couldn't help but feel a surge of optimism for the future. With their collective efforts and dedication, she was confident that BrightTech would continue to thrive in a culture of excellence, driven by a performance management paradigm that put its employees at the forefront of success.

With the performance appraisal forms finalized, Emma knew that conducting appraisal meetings would be the next crucial step in the implementation process. As she gathered her team once again, she emphasized the importance of following best practices to ensure that the appraisal meetings were conducted effectively and professionally.

"Performance appraisal meetings are an opportunity for meaningful dialogue and reflection," Emma began, her voice steady and commanding. "We need to approach these meetings with empathy, openness, and a genuine desire to support our employees in their growth and development."

Together, they discussed the key elements of conducting successful appraisal meetings, drawing on best practices and lessons learned from their research and experiences. Emma stressed the importance of preparation, encouraging managers to review the employee's performance appraisal form beforehand and come to the meeting with specific examples and observations to share.

"Preparation is key to ensuring that the appraisal meeting is focused and productive," Emma explained. "Managers should be ready to provide specific feedback, discuss performance expectations, and collaboratively set goals for the future."

As they delved deeper into the discussion, Emma emphasized the importance of active listening and empathy during the appraisal meetings. She encouraged managers to create a supportive and non-judgmental environment where employees feel comfortable expressing themselves and sharing their perspectives.

"Listening is just as important as talking during these meetings," Emma reminded them. "We need to be attentive to our employees' concerns, acknowledge their achievements, and offer constructive feedback that will help them grow and improve."

Finally, Emma stressed the importance of follow-up and ongoing support after the appraisal meetings. She encouraged managers to schedule regular check-ins with their employees to monitor progress, provide additional support or resources as needed, and ensure that performance goals are being met.

"Performance management is not a one-time event—it's an

ongoing process," Emma reminded them. "By continuing to support and empower our employees, we can ensure that they have the tools and resources they need to succeed."

As the meeting drew to a close, Emma felt a sense of pride and confidence in her team. With their commitment to following best practices and their dedication to supporting their employees, she knew that they were well-equipped to conduct successful performance appraisal meetings and drive continued excellence at BrightTech.

6

Chapter Six: Performance Recognition and Rewards

With the foundation of the new performance management system laid, Emma turned her attention to the crucial aspect of recognizing and rewarding employees for their outstanding contributions. She knew that building a culture of excellence required more than just setting goals and providing feedback—it also required celebrating achievements and fostering a sense of appreciation and gratitude among the team.

As Emma gathered her colleagues for a strategy session, she emphasized the importance of designing a comprehensive recognition and rewards program that would motivate and inspire employees to perform at their best. Together, they brainstormed ideas and explored various approaches to recognizing and rewarding outstanding performance.

"Recognition is about more than just monetary rewards," Emma explained, her voice filled with passion and conviction. "It's about acknowledging the hard work, dedication, and achievements of our employees in meaningful and personalized ways."

They discussed the importance of both formal and informal recognition, including everything from public shout-outs during team meetings to personalized notes of appreciation from managers. Emma stressed the value of celebrating both individual and team achievements, fostering a sense of camaraderie and collaboration among colleagues.

"Recognition should be timely, specific, and sincere," Emma emphasized. "It should be tied directly to the behaviors and outcomes we want to encourage, and it should make employees feel valued and appreciated for their contributions."

As they continued to brainstorm ideas, Emma introduced the concept of rewards and incentives as a way to further motivate and incentivize high performance. They discussed various types of rewards, including bonuses, gift cards, extra paid time off, and opportunities for career development and advancement.

"Rewards should be aligned with our organizational values and goals," Emma explained. "They should reinforce desired behaviors and outcomes, and they should be meaningful and relevant to the individual employee."

Together, they developed a comprehensive recognition and rewards program that encompassed both formal and informal recognition, as well as a variety of rewards and incentives to suit the diverse needs and preferences of their employees. Emma felt a sense of excitement and optimism as they finalized the program, knowing that it would play a crucial role in fostering a culture of excellence and driving continued success at BrightTech.

As they concluded the meeting, Emma couldn't help but feel a sense of pride in what they had accomplished together. With their new performance management system and comprehensive recognition and rewards program in place, she knew that BrightTech was well-positioned to achieve even greater heights of success in the future.

As Emma and her team finalized the details of the recognition and rewards program, they delved deeper into the importance of these initiatives in driving performance and fostering a culture of excellence within BrightTech. Emma knew that recognition and rewards were not just nice gestures—they were powerful tools for motivating employees, increasing engagement, and ultimately driving business success.

"Recognition is the fuel that powers employee engagement and motivation," Emma explained passionately to her colleagues. "When employees feel appreciated and valued for their contributions, they are more likely to go above and beyond to achieve success."

She shared anecdotes of past experiences where a simple word of appreciation or a small token of recognition had made a significant impact on employee morale and performance. She emphasized that recognition didn't have to be grandiose to be effective—it just needed to be genuine and heartfelt.

"Recognition is about acknowledging the little things as much as the big achievements," Emma continued. "It's about celebrating progress, effort, and improvement, not just the end results."

Her words resonated with her team, and they nodded in agreement, realizing the profound impact that meaningful recognition could have on employee motivation and performance.

"Rewards, on the other hand, are about incentivizing and reinforcing desired behaviors and outcomes," Emma explained.

"They provide employees with tangible incentives for their hard work and dedication, and they can help drive a culture of high performance and accountability."

She stressed the importance of aligning rewards with organizational goals and values, ensuring that they incentivized behaviors and outcomes that were conducive to the company's success.

"By combining both recognition and rewards, we can create a powerful system that motivates and inspires employees to perform at their best," Emma concluded. "And in doing so, we can build a culture of excellence where every employee feels valued, empowered, and motivated to contribute to the company's success."

With a renewed sense of purpose and determination, Emma and her team finalized the recognition and rewards program, knowing that it would play a pivotal role in driving performance and fostering a culture of excellence at BrightTech.

With the recognition and rewards program taking shape, Emma and her team delved into the different types of recognition programs they could implement at BrightTech. They understood that a one-size-fits-all approach wouldn't work, so they brainstormed a variety of options to cater to the diverse needs and preferences of their employees.

"Monetary rewards are often seen as the gold standard of recognition programs," Emma explained, pacing the room as she spoke. "They provide employees with tangible incentives for their hard work and achievements, such as bonuses, salary increases, or profit-sharing."

She highlighted the importance of aligning monetary rewards with performance goals and outcomes, ensuring that they were both meaningful and motivating for employees. However, she also acknowledged that monetary rewards weren't always feasible or sustainable for every organization.

"Non-monetary rewards, on the other hand, can be just as effective in motivating and engaging employees," Emma continued. "These can include things like public recognition, praise from managers, opportunities for career advancement, or even extra time off."

She emphasized that non-monetary rewards could often be more personal and meaningful than their monetary counterparts, as they tapped into employees' intrinsic motivations and sense of fulfillment.

"Ultimately, the key is to strike a balance between monetary and non-monetary rewards, depending on the preferences and needs of our employees," Emma concluded. "By offering a diverse range of recognition programs, we can ensure that every employee feels valued and appreciated for their contributions to the company."

With a clear understanding of the different types of recognition programs available, Emma and her team set out to design a comprehensive program that would celebrate the achievements of BrightTech employees and drive a culture of excellence and innovation within the organization.

Amidst the excitement of designing the recognition and rewards program, Emma paused to address a critical aspect: ensuring fairness and equity in reward distribution. She knew that without fairness, the entire program could unravel, leading to resentment and disengagement among employees.

Gathering her team in the conference room, Emma began, her tone serious yet determined. "One of our top priorities in designing this program is to ensure that it's fair and equitable for all employees. We must be vigilant in avoiding biases and favoritism."

She stressed the importance of establishing clear criteria and transparent processes for reward distribution, ensuring that every employee had an equal opportunity to be recognized and rewarded for their contributions.

"We need to guard against any unconscious biases that may influence our decision-making," Emma continued. "Whether it's gender, race, or personal relationships, we must remain objective and impartial in our assessments."

To achieve this, Emma proposed implementing a review process where multiple stakeholders would provide input and feedback on reward decisions, mitigating the risk of individual biases.

"Transparency is key," Emma emphasized. "Employees need to understand how rewards are determined and feel confident that the process is fair and consistent across the board."

With a firm commitment to fairness and equity, Emma and her team set out to implement safeguards and mechanisms to ensure that the recognition and rewards program would uphold these principles, fostering a culture of trust and inclusivity within BrightTech.

7

Chapter Seven: Training and Development for Performance Improvement

As Emma's journey to transform BrightTech continued, she recognized that to sustain the culture of excellence she had cultivated, investing in training and development was paramount. With the foundation of a robust performance management system in place, Emma knew that empowering employees with the right skills and knowledge would further drive organizational success.

Gathering her team in the boardroom, Emma's voice resonated with determination. "Training and development are not just investments in our employees; they are investments in the future of BrightTech. We must equip our workforce with the skills they need to adapt, innovate, and excel in an ever-evolving business landscape."

She outlined a comprehensive training program that encompassed technical skills, leadership development, and soft skills enhancement. "We need to provide targeted training programs tailored to the needs of different departments and roles," Emma emphasized. "Whether it's technical certifications, leadership workshops, or communication skills training, every employee should have access to opportunities for growth and development."

Recognizing that traditional training methods might not suffice in today's fast-paced world, Emma proposed leveraging technology to deliver personalized and engaging learning experiences. "We can utilize online learning platforms, virtual reality simulations, and gamified training modules to make learning more accessible and enjoyable for our employees," she explained.

But Emma's vision went beyond just acquiring new skills; it was about fostering a culture of continuous learning and improvement. "Training and development should not be viewed as one-time events but as ongoing processes," she said. "We need to instill a mindset of curiosity and self-improvement among our employees, encouraging them to seek out learning opportunities and grow both personally and professionally."

With unwavering determination, Emma and her team embarked on the next phase of their journey, confident that investing in training and development would not only enhance individual performance but also propel BrightTech to new heights of success.

As Emma delved deeper into the intricacies of revamping BrightTech's performance management system, she realized the critical role that identifying training needs based on performance evaluations played in fostering employee growth and development.

Gathering her team once more, Emma emphasized the importance of aligning training initiatives with the specific needs identified through performance evaluations. "Our performance appraisals provide invaluable insights into areas where employees excel and areas where they may need additional support," she explained. "By leveraging this data, we can tailor our training programs to address individual and team-level skill gaps."

With determination in her voice, Emma led her team through a detailed analysis of the latest performance evaluation results. They identified trends and patterns, pinpointing common areas for improvement across departments. "From technical proficiency to leadership competencies, our performance evaluations shed light on the skills and capabilities that will drive our organization forward," Emma declared.

Armed with this knowledge, Emma and her team meticulously crafted a training roadmap that addressed the identified needs. They curated a diverse range of learning experiences, from specialized workshops to mentorship programs, designed to empower employees to reach their full potential.

But Emma knew that the success of their training initiatives hinged not only on content but also on delivery. "We need to ensure that our training programs are not only informative but also engaging and accessible," she insisted. "Whether it's through interactive online modules or hands-on workshops, we must cater to diverse learning styles and preferences."

With a clear plan in place, Emma and her team set out to implement their tailored training programs, confident that by leveraging performance evaluations to identify training needs, they were laying the foundation for a culture of continuous learning and improvement at BrightTech.

With the roadmap for training needs laid out, Emma dove into the task of designing and delivering effective training programs. She knew that the success of these programs would be crucial in driving performance improvement and fostering a culture of excellence at BrightTech.

Gathering her team in the vibrant conference room, Emma began brainstorming ideas for the training programs. "We need to make these programs impactful and engaging," she emphasized. "They should not only address the identified skill gaps but also inspire our employees to strive for greatness."

As ideas flowed, Emma scribbled notes furiously, capturing the essence of each suggestion. From interactive workshops led by industry experts to immersive simulations that mirrored real-world scenarios, the possibilities seemed endless. "We have a diverse workforce with varying learning styles," Emma noted. "Our training programs must cater to everyone, from the fresh graduates to the seasoned professionals."

With the framework in place, Emma tasked her team with fleshing out the details of each program. They meticulously curated content, ensuring it was relevant, practical, and aligned with the organization's goals. "Our training materials should not only impart knowledge but also inspire action," Emma remarked. "We want our employees to walk away feeling empowered and motivated to apply what they've learned."

But designing the programs was only half the battle. Emma knew that delivery was equally crucial in ensuring their effectiveness. "We need dynamic facilitators who can captivate our audience and create an immersive learning experience," she declared. "Our training sessions should be interactive, thought-provoking, and above all, impactful."

As the training programs took shape, Emma felt a surge of excitement. She envisioned the positive impact they would have on BrightTech's employees, equipping them with the skills and knowledge needed to excel in their roles. With determination in her heart, Emma knew that these programs would be instrumental in propelling BrightTech towards a future of unparalleled success and innovation.

As the training programs were rolled out across BrightTech, Emma knew that measuring their impact on performance improvement was essential. She gathered her team once more, ready to tackle this critical aspect of their initiative.

"We need to ensure that our training efforts translate into tangible improvements in performance," Emma declared, her voice filled with determination. "We must have mechanisms in place to assess the effectiveness of our programs and identify areas for further enhancement."

Her team nodded in agreement, recognizing the importance of this next step. They brainstormed various methods for measuring the impact of training on performance, from traditional assessments to more innovative approaches.

"We can conduct pre- and post-training assessments to gauge the knowledge gained and skills developed," suggested one team member. "Additionally, we could track key performance indicators before and after training to measure any improvements."

Emma nodded in approval, jotting down their ideas on a whiteboard. "But it's not just about the numbers," she added. "We also need to gather qualitative feedback from employees to understand their perception of the training and its practical application in their roles."

With a plan in place, Emma and her team set out to implement their measurement strategy. They worked tirelessly to collect data, analyze results, and draw insights into the impact of the training programs.

As the findings began to emerge, Emma felt a sense of validation. The data showed significant improvements in employee performance across various departments. Productivity soared, error rates decreased, and employee satisfaction reached new heights.

But Emma wasn't content with just numbers on a report. She delved deeper, conducting interviews and focus groups to uncover the human stories behind the statistics. She listened intently as employees shared their experiences, detailing how the training had empowered them to tackle challenges with confidence and creativity.

Armed with this feedback, Emma refined the training programs further, addressing any areas for improvement and building on their successes. She knew that the journey towards building a culture of excellence was ongoing, but with each step forward, BrightTech was one step closer to unlocking its full potential.

8

Chapter Eight: Technology in Performance Management

With the foundation of a dynamic performance management system in place, Emma knew that integrating cutting-edge technology was crucial to sustain and enhance their progress. As she gathered her team to discuss the next phase of their journey, excitement filled the room.

"Technology will be our ally in revolutionizing performance management at BrightTech," Emma declared, her eyes shining with determination. "It will enable us to streamline processes, gather real-time data, and empower employees like never before."

The team nodded in agreement, eager to explore the possibilities that technology could offer. They brainstormed ideas for leveraging technology in performance management, from implementing cloud-based platforms for performance reviews to developing mobile apps for continuous feedback.

But as they delved deeper into their discussions, they encountered challenges. Some team members expressed concerns about data security and privacy, while others worried about the potential for technological solutions to be biased or discriminatory.

Emma listened attentively to their concerns, recognizing the importance of addressing them head-on. "We must prioritize transparency and fairness in our use of technology," she asserted. "We'll work closely with our IT department to ensure that our systems are secure, compliant, and free from bias."

With a plan in place to mitigate these risks, Emma and her team forged ahead with their technological initiatives. They collaborated closely with IT experts to select and implement the right tools and systems, customizing them to meet the unique needs of BrightTech.

As the new technology was rolled out across the organization, Emma witnessed its transformative impact firsthand. Performance reviews became more efficient and data-driven, thanks to automated processes and real-time analytics. Employees embraced mobile feedback apps, using them to provide and receive continuous guidance and recognition.

But perhaps most importantly, the new technology fostered a culture of transparency and collaboration at BrightTech. Employees felt empowered to take ownership of their performance and development, leveraging technology as a tool for growth and success.

As Emma reflected on their journey, she knew that technology was not just a means to an end but a catalyst for change. With the right tools and mindset, BrightTech was poised to continue its evolution towards a culture of excellence and innovation. And Emma was proud to have played a part in shaping that future.

As Emma and her team embarked on their journey to

revolutionize performance management at BrightTech, they knew that harnessing the power of technology was key to their success. With determination in her eyes, Emma led the charge to automate outdated processes and streamline their performance management framework.

"Technology will be our ally in transforming the way we manage performance," Emma declared to her team, her voice ringing with conviction. "We'll leverage automation to eliminate manual tasks, reduce errors, and free up valuable time for more meaningful work."

With that vision in mind, they set out to identify areas where technology could make the most impact. They mapped out the performance management process from start to finish, pinpointing inefficiencies and pain points along the way.

"It's time to bid farewell to cumbersome spreadsheets and paperwork," Emma announced, as the team gathered around a whiteboard filled with diagrams and flowcharts. "With the right technology, we can digitize our processes and make them more efficient and user-friendly."

Their first task was to implement an automated performance review system. They collaborated with IT experts to select a user-friendly platform that could handle complex workflows, customizable templates, and real-time feedback mechanisms.

As the new system was rolled out, Emma marveled at its transformative power. Performance reviews that once took weeks to complete now took mere days, thanks to automated reminders and streamlined approval processes. Employees embraced the intuitive interface, using it to set goals, track progress, and provide feedback in real-time.

But the benefits of automation didn't stop there. With data flowing seamlessly between systems, Emma and her team gained valuable insights into employee performance trends and patterns. They could identify areas for improvement more quickly and make data-driven decisions to drive organizational success.

As Emma reflected on their progress, she knew that technology was not just a tool but a catalyst for change. With automation at the heart of their performance management system, BrightTech was poised to thrive in a new era of efficiency and innovation. And Emma was proud to have led the charge.

With the vision of revolutionizing performance management at BrightTech firmly in mind, Emma and her team faced a critical decision: choosing the right performance management software to support their ambitious goals.

As they gathered in the conference room, Emma spread out brochures and product demos, each promising to be the solution they were looking for. But Emma knew that this decision couldn't be made lightly. The software they chose would shape the future of performance management at BrightTech for years to come.

"We need a solution that is not only robust and user-friendly but also scalable and customizable to meet our unique needs," Emma emphasized, her voice commanding attention.

The team poured over the options, weighing the pros and cons of each software platform. They considered factors such as ease of implementation, integration capabilities, and ongoing support services.

"It's not just about finding the software with the most bells and whistles," Emma reminded them. "We need a partner who will work with us every step of the way, understanding our challenges and helping us achieve our goals."

After hours of deliberation and spirited debate, they finally reached a consensus. They selected a performance management software provider known for its innovative solutions and customer-centric approach.

With the decision made, Emma wasted no time in reaching out to the software vendor to begin the implementation process. She worked closely with their team to customize the platform to BrightTech's specific requirements, ensuring a seamless transition for employees.

As the weeks passed and the new software took shape, Emma felt a sense of excitement building within the team. They were on the brink of ushering in a new era of performance management at BrightTech, one powered by cutting-edge technology and fueled by their shared vision of excellence.

With the right performance management software in place, Emma knew that BrightTech was poised to achieve greatness. And she couldn't wait to see the transformative impact it would have on the organization and its employees.

As Emma and her team embarked on the journey to modernize BrightTech's performance management system, they faced another crucial challenge: integrating it seamlessly with the company's existing HR systems.

Gathered around the conference table once more, Emma discussed the importance of this integration. "We need our performance management system to work in harmony with our HRIS, learning management, and payroll systems," she emphasized.

The team nodded in agreement, understanding the significance of creating a cohesive ecosystem that would streamline processes and enhance the employee experience.

But as they delved deeper into the technical aspects of integration, they encountered roadblocks and complexities they hadn't anticipated. Legacy systems, data silos, and incompatible platforms threatened to derail their progress.

Emma refused to be deterred. With her characteristic determination, she rallied the team to find innovative solutions to overcome these obstacles.

"We need to think outside the box," she declared. "We can't let outdated technology hold us back from achieving our goals."

Drawing on their collective expertise, the team brainstormed creative approaches to integration. They explored API connections, data migration strategies, and custom development solutions, determined to find the most efficient and effective way forward.

After weeks of intensive collaboration and problem-solving, they finally had a breakthrough. They developed a comprehensive integration plan that would seamlessly link BrightTech's performance management system with its other HR systems, allowing for real-time data exchange and a unified employee experience.

With the integration plan in place, Emma and her team set to work implementing it, meticulously testing each component to ensure reliability and accuracy.

As the final pieces fell into place and the integration went live, Emma felt a surge of satisfaction. BrightTech now had a fully integrated performance management ecosystem, empowering employees and managers alike to drive success and achieve their full potential.

With this critical milestone behind them, Emma knew that BrightTech was well-positioned to continue its journey toward building a culture of excellence—one that embraced technology as a catalyst for positive change and growth.

9

Chapter Nine: Performance Management for Remote and Distributed Teams

As Emma celebrated the successful implementation of BrightTech's revamped performance management system, she faced a new challenge: how to adapt the system to meet the needs of remote and distributed teams.

Gathering her team once again, Emma addressed the pressing issue head-on. "With the rise of remote work, we need to ensure that our performance management system is equipped to support our dispersed teams effectively," she declared.

The team nodded in agreement, recognizing the importance of maintaining performance standards and fostering engagement, regardless of employees' locations.

Emma knew that traditional performance management practices, such as in-person meetings and face-to-face feedback sessions, wouldn't suffice in this new remote environment. They needed innovative solutions tailored to the unique dynamics of remote work.

Drawing on her expertise and experience, Emma proposed a multifaceted approach to address the challenges of managing remote and distributed teams.

"We need to leverage technology to facilitate communication, collaboration, and feedback," she explained. "But we also need to focus on building trust, establishing clear expectations, and providing ongoing support."

The team brainstormed ideas for enhancing communication and collaboration among remote team members. They explored the use of virtual collaboration tools, such as video conferencing platforms and project management software, to facilitate real-time communication and document sharing.

But they also recognized the importance of fostering a sense of belonging and camaraderie among remote employees. They proposed virtual team-building activities, online social events, and remote-friendly recognition programs to strengthen bonds and boost morale.

As they delved deeper into their discussions, Emma and her team identified key strategies for managing performance in a remote environment:

1. Setting clear goals and expectations: Ensuring that remote employees understand their roles, responsibilities, and performance objectives from the outset.
2. Providing regular feedback and coaching: Establishing regular check-ins and one-on-one meetings to provide feedback, offer support, and address any performance issues promptly.
3. Leveraging technology for performance tracking: Utilizing performance management software to track progress, monitor performance metrics, and identify areas for

improvement.
4. Encouraging self-assessment and reflection: Empowering remote employees to take ownership of their performance through self-assessment exercises and reflection activities.
5. Recognizing and rewarding remote achievements: Implementing virtual recognition programs and rewards to celebrate the accomplishments of remote team members and foster a culture of appreciation.

Armed with these strategies, Emma and her team set out to adapt BrightTech's performance management system to meet the needs of its remote workforce. They knew that by embracing innovation and creativity, they could continue to drive success and excellence in this new era of remote work.

As Emma and her team delved deeper into the challenges of managing performance in remote work environments, they uncovered a host of unique obstacles that required innovative solutions.

"Remote work presents a whole new set of challenges for performance management," Emma remarked, her brow furrowed in thought. "We need to address issues like communication barriers, feelings of isolation, and the blurring of work-life boundaries."

Her team nodded in agreement, each member recalling their own experiences with remote work challenges.

"Communication is key," one team member chimed in. "Without the ability to walk over to someone's desk and ask a quick question, remote employees can feel disconnected and out of the loop."

Emma nodded thoughtfully. "We'll need to find ways to facilitate communication and collaboration, whether it's through scheduled video calls, instant messaging platforms, or virtual team meetings."

Another team member raised a concern about maintaining productivity in remote settings. "Without the structure of a traditional office environment, some employees may struggle to stay focused and motivated," they explained.

Emma acknowledged the validity of their concern. "We'll need to provide remote employees with the tools and resources they need to succeed, whether it's access to training programs, productivity apps, or ergonomic workstations."

The team also discussed the importance of addressing feelings of isolation and loneliness among remote employees. "Working from home can be isolating, especially for employees who live alone or are accustomed to a bustling office environment," one team member observed.

Emma nodded sympathetically. "We'll need to prioritize employee well-being and mental health by offering virtual wellness programs, social events, and opportunities for team bonding."

As they brainstormed solutions to these unique challenges, Emma and her team remained focused on their ultimate goal: building a culture of excellence and empowerment, even in the face of remote work obstacles. They knew that by embracing change and adapting to new realities, they could continue to drive success and innovation in the ever-evolving world of remote work.

As Emma and her team continued their exploration of performance management for remote and distributed teams, they turned their attention to strategies for effectively monitoring and evaluating remote team performance.

"With remote work becoming more prevalent, it's crucial that we have robust methods in place for monitoring and evaluating performance," Emma emphasized, her voice resonating with determination.

Her team nodded in agreement, eager to tackle this new challenge head-on.

"We need to establish clear performance expectations and goals for remote employees," one team member suggested. "This will provide a framework for assessing their progress and contributions."

Emma nodded in agreement. "But we also need to recognize that traditional metrics may not fully capture the complexities of remote work. We'll need to take a more holistic approach, considering factors like adaptability, communication skills, and the ability to work independently."

Another team member raised a concern about maintaining accountability in remote settings. "Without direct supervision, some employees may feel tempted to slack off or become disengaged," they pointed out.

Emma acknowledged the validity of their concern. "That's why it's important to establish regular check-ins and performance reviews," she explained. "These meetings will provide opportunities for feedback, goal-setting, and course correction as needed."

The team also discussed the importance of leveraging technology to monitor remote team performance. "We can use tools like project management software, time-tracking apps, and performance dashboards to track progress and identify areas for improvement," one team member suggested.

Emma nodded in agreement. "Technology will play a key role in ensuring transparency, accountability, and efficiency in our remote work initiatives."

As they brainstormed strategies for effectively monitoring and evaluating remote team performance, Emma and her team remained committed to their mission of building a culture of excellence and empowerment, even in the ever-evolving landscape of remote work. They knew that by embracing innovation and adaptability, they could continue to drive success and inspire greatness in their distributed workforce.

As Emma and her team continued their discussion on performance management for remote and distributed teams, they delved into the subpoint of leveraging technology for remote performance management.

"Technology will be our greatest ally in navigating the challenges of managing remote teams," Emma declared, her voice resolute with determination.

Her team members nodded in agreement, recognizing the importance of harnessing technology to streamline remote performance management processes.

"We need tools that allow us to effectively communicate, collaborate, and monitor performance from anywhere in the world," one team member suggested.

Emma nodded, her mind already racing with ideas. "Indeed. We should explore platforms that offer features such as video conferencing, instant messaging, document sharing, and real-time collaboration."

Another team member raised a concern about the potential for technology to feel impersonal in remote work environments. "How do we ensure that our use of technology doesn't detract from the human connection and sense of camaraderie among team members?" they asked.

Emma paused, considering the question thoughtfully. "While technology will certainly be a key enabler of remote performance management, we must also prioritize human-centric approaches," she explained. "This means fostering open communication, providing opportunities for virtual team-building activities, and promoting a culture of empathy and support."

The team nodded in agreement, reassured by Emma's emphasis on maintaining the human element in their remote work initiatives.

As they brainstormed ways to leverage technology for remote performance management, Emma and her team remained focused on their ultimate goal: building a culture of excellence and empowerment, even in the face of unprecedented challenges. They knew that by harnessing the power of technology while staying true to their values, they could lead their organization to new heights of success in the remote work era.

10

Chapter Ten: Performance Management for Different Organizational Structures

As Emma and her team celebrated the successful implementation of the new performance management system, they knew there was still work to be done. The next challenge on their journey to building a culture of excellence was adapting performance management to suit the diverse organizational structures within the company.

Emma gathered her team in the conference room, the air buzzing with anticipation. They knew that navigating the complexities of various organizational structures would require careful planning and strategic thinking.

"Each department within our organization operates differently, with its own unique set of goals, processes, and challenges," Emma began, her voice steady and determined. "To ensure the success of our performance management system, we must tailor our approach to accommodate these differences."

The team nodded in agreement, ready to tackle this new

challenge head-on.

"We need to consider factors such as hierarchy, decision-making processes, and communication channels," Emma continued. "By understanding the intricacies of each organizational structure, we can design performance management strategies that align with the needs and objectives of each department."

One team member raised a concern about the potential for resistance to change within certain departments. "Some teams may be more resistant to adopting new performance management practices," they pointed out. "How do we ensure buy-in from all levels of the organization?"

Emma smiled, her confidence unwavering. "Change is never easy, but it's essential for growth and progress," she replied. "We will need to communicate effectively, provide ample support and training, and demonstrate the benefits of the new system to win over skeptics."

The team listened intently, reassured by Emma's unwavering leadership.

As they brainstormed strategies for adapting performance management to different organizational structures, Emma and her team remained focused on their ultimate goal: building a culture of excellence that empowered employees and drove organizational success.

With determination and creativity, they knew they could overcome any challenge that stood in their way and continue to lead their organization to new heights of success.

In the heart of the corporate headquarters, Emma and her team gathered once more to address the nuanced challenge of tailoring performance management systems to fit the diverse organizational structures within the company.

With charts and graphs spread across the table, Emma dove

into the discussion. "Hierarchical and flat organizational structures require different approaches to performance management," she explained, her voice resonating with authority. "In hierarchical structures, clear lines of authority and reporting are prevalent, making traditional performance evaluation methods more suitable."

She glanced around the room, ensuring everyone was following along. "However, in flat organizational structures, where decision-making is decentralized and employees have more autonomy, we need to adopt more flexible and collaborative performance management practices."

A team member raised their hand, eager to contribute. "How do we ensure fairness and consistency in performance evaluations across different organizational structures?" they asked, voicing a concern shared by many.

Emma nodded, acknowledging the importance of their question. "Consistency is key," she replied, her gaze unwavering. "We must establish clear evaluation criteria and ensure that managers across all departments adhere to the same standards."

As the discussion unfolded, Emma and her team brainstormed innovative solutions to the challenges posed by hierarchical and flat organizational structures. They recognized that while each structure presented its own set of complexities, with careful planning and strategic implementation, they could design performance management systems that would drive success across the entire organization.

With renewed determination, Emma and her team forged ahead, confident that they were one step closer to achieving their goal of building a culture of excellence that would propel the company to new heights of success.

In the vast meeting room of the corporate headquarters,

CHAPTER TEN: PERFORMANCE MANAGEMENT FOR DIFFERENT...

Emma and her team delved into the intricate challenge of adapting performance management practices for matrix organizations, where employees report to multiple managers and work across different teams.

Emma stood at the front of the room, her eyes focused and her voice resolute. "Matrix organizations require a flexible approach to performance management," she began, her words echoing with authority. "Traditional hierarchical structures won't suffice here."

She glanced around the room, meeting the eyes of each team member. "In matrix organizations, we must prioritize collaboration, cross-functional teamwork, and agility," she continued, emphasizing each point with a firm nod.

A team member raised their hand, seeking clarification. "How do we ensure accountability and clarity in performance expectations when employees are reporting to multiple managers?" they inquired, voicing a concern shared by many.

Emma paused, considering the question carefully before responding. "Communication is key," she replied, her voice unwavering. "We need to establish clear lines of communication between managers and employees, ensure alignment on performance goals, and foster open dialogue to address any challenges that may arise."

As the discussion unfolded, Emma and her team brainstormed innovative solutions to the complexities of performance management in matrix organizations. They recognized the need for agility, adaptability, and strong communication channels to navigate the unique dynamics of this organizational structure.

With renewed determination, Emma and her team forged ahead, confident that they were on the right path to designing performance management systems that would thrive in the dynamic environment of matrix organizations. They knew that by embracing change and leveraging the power of collaboration, they could build a culture of excellence that would propel the company to new heights of success.

In a conference room adorned with flags from various countries, Emma and her team gathered to tackle the challenge of addressing cultural differences in performance management. They recognized that in a multinational corporation like theirs, cultural nuances could significantly impact the effectiveness of performance management practices.

Emma stood at the head of the table, her gaze sweeping across the room. "We must acknowledge and embrace the diversity of cultures within our organization," she declared, her voice carrying the weight of conviction. "What works in one country may not work in another, and it's our responsibility to adapt our performance management approach accordingly."

A hush fell over the room as Emma continued, her words resonating with the gravity of the task at hand. "We need to conduct thorough research into the cultural norms and values of each country where we operate," she explained. "By understanding and respecting these differences, we can tailor our performance management practices to align with local expectations and preferences."

As the discussion unfolded, team members shared insights and experiences from their respective regions, offering valuable perspectives on how cultural differences could impact performance management. They brainstormed innovative strategies to bridge cultural divides, foster inclusivity, and ensure fairness and equity in performance evaluation processes.

Emma listened intently to each contribution, synthesizing the diverse viewpoints into a cohesive plan of action. She knew that by embracing cultural diversity and leveraging it as a strength rather than a challenge, they could create a performance management system that resonated with employees across the globe.

Armed with a newfound understanding of the importance of cultural sensitivity in performance management, Emma and her team left the meeting room with a renewed sense of purpose. They were determined to pave the way for a culture of excellence that celebrated diversity, fostered inclusivity, and empowered employees to thrive regardless of their cultural background.

11

Chapter Eleven: Legal and Ethical considerations in Performance Management

As Emma delved deeper into the overhaul of the performance management system, she encountered a labyrinth of legal and ethical considerations that threatened to derail their progress. In a tense meeting with the legal team, Emma listened intently as they outlined the potential pitfalls and risks associated with performance management practices.

"We must ensure that our performance evaluation criteria are fair, transparent, and non-discriminatory," the chief legal counsel emphasized, her voice echoing through the boardroom. "Any hint of bias or unfair treatment could expose us to lawsuits and damage our reputation."

Emma nodded thoughtfully, acutely aware of the gravity of their discussion. She knew that navigating the legal landscape would require meticulous attention to detail and a steadfast commitment to upholding ethical standards.

"We also need to consider data privacy regulations," another legal expert chimed in, her brow furrowed with concern. "Collecting and storing employee performance data comes with significant legal implications, especially in light of recent data protection laws."

Emma's mind raced as she processed the myriad legal and ethical challenges that lay ahead. She understood that protecting employee privacy and confidentiality was paramount, but she also recognized the need to gather meaningful performance data to drive organizational success.

With the weight of legal and ethical considerations bearing down on her, Emma resolved to forge ahead with caution and integrity. She knew that by working closely with the legal team and adhering to stringent ethical standards, they could navigate the complexities of performance management while safeguarding the rights and well-being of their employees.

Armed with a newfound understanding of the legal and ethical landscape, Emma and her team embarked on the next phase of their journey, fortified by a steadfast commitment to excellence and integrity.

As Emma delved deeper into the legal and ethical considerations of performance management, she knew that compliance with relevant employment laws and regulations was non-negotiable. In a dimly lit conference room, she sat across from a team of legal experts, poring over stacks of documents outlining the intricacies of labor laws and regulations.

"We need to ensure that our performance management practices comply with all relevant employment laws," one of the legal experts emphasized, her tone firm and unwavering.

Emma nodded in agreement, her mind racing as she processed the implications of their discussion. She understood that failure to comply with employment laws could result in costly lawsuits, damage to the company's reputation, and even legal penalties.

"We must pay close attention to laws regarding discrimination, harassment, and retaliation," another legal expert chimed in, her voice echoing with urgency. "These laws protect our employees' rights and must be upheld at all times."

Emma felt a sense of responsibility weighing heavily on her shoulders as she absorbed the gravity of their conversation. She knew that compliance with employment laws was not just a legal obligation but a moral imperative.

With determination and resolve, Emma vowed to meticulously review every aspect of the performance management system to ensure it aligned with the requirements of employment laws and regulations. She knew that by prioritizing compliance, they could build a culture of excellence rooted in integrity and respect for employee rights.

Armed with a newfound commitment to compliance, Emma and her team embarked on the arduous task of navigating the legal landscape, knowing that their efforts would lay the foundation for a performance management system that upheld the highest standards of legality and ethics.

In the heart of the HR department, Emma sat surrounded by her team, grappling with the critical issue of ensuring fairness and non-discrimination in the performance management processes. The weight of responsibility hung heavy in the air as they delved into the complexities of this crucial task.

"We need to ensure that our performance management processes are fair and free from any form of discrimination," Emma asserted, her voice firm with determination.

Her team nodded in agreement, understanding the profound

impact that fairness and equality would have on the organization's culture and reputation.

"We must implement rigorous training programs to educate managers and employees on the importance of fair and unbiased performance evaluations," one team member suggested, her eyes alight with conviction.

Emma seized upon the idea, recognizing the importance of equipping employees with the knowledge and tools to recognize and address any instances of bias or discrimination.

"We also need to establish clear guidelines and criteria for performance evaluation to ensure consistency and transparency," another team member added, her words echoing with purpose.

Emma nodded in agreement, knowing that transparency and consistency were essential pillars of a fair and effective performance management system.

With a renewed sense of purpose, Emma and her team embarked on the task of designing and implementing robust training programs and establishing clear guidelines to promote fairness and non-discrimination in every aspect of the performance management process.

As they worked tirelessly to uphold these principles, Emma knew that their efforts would not only transform the organization's performance management practices but also foster a culture of equality, respect, and excellence for years to come.

In the dimly lit conference room, Emma and her team huddled together, grappling with the weighty issue of protecting employee privacy and confidentiality in the realm of performance management. The air was heavy with tension as they delved into the intricate legal and ethical considerations.

"We need to ensure that employee privacy is safeguarded at every step of the performance management process," Emma declared, her voice carrying a note of urgency.

Her team members nodded in agreement, fully cognizant of the delicate balance between transparency and confidentiality.

"We must establish robust protocols for handling sensitive employee data, ensuring that only authorized personnel have access," one team member suggested, her brow furrowed in concentration.

Emma seized upon the idea, recognizing the paramount importance of implementing stringent security measures to prevent unauthorized access to confidential information.

"We also need to educate employees about their rights regarding privacy and confidentiality," another team member added, her tone resolute.

Emma nodded in agreement, knowing that empowering employees with knowledge would bolster their trust in the organization and its commitment to protecting their privacy.

With a sense of purpose, Emma and her team set out to develop comprehensive training programs and stringent protocols to safeguard employee privacy and confidentiality. They knew that their efforts would not only uphold the organization's legal and ethical obligations but also foster a culture of trust, respect, and integrity.

As they worked tirelessly to fortify these safeguards, Emma felt a sense of pride.

12

Chapter Twelve: Continuous Improvement of Performance Management Systems

In the heart of the bustling corporate headquarters, Emma convened a meeting of her team, a group now seasoned by trials and triumphs. They gathered around a table strewn with documents and charts, a testament to their collective journey of transformation.

"Our journey doesn't end here," Emma declared, her voice resolute as she looked around at her colleagues, each one brimming with determination. "Continuous improvement is the key to sustaining our success."

Her words sparked a fervor among the team, igniting a shared commitment to never settle for the status quo.

"We must remain vigilant in monitoring the effectiveness of our performance management system," Emma continued, her eyes alight with fervent passion. "We must adapt and evolve to meet the ever-changing needs of our organization and its employees."

With renewed zeal, Emma and her team embarked on a mission of continuous improvement. They analyzed data, solicited feedback, and conducted thorough evaluations to identify areas of strength and areas in need of enhancement.

"We need to stay ahead of the curve," one team member proclaimed, echoing the sentiments of the group.

With that mantra in mind, Emma and her team explored innovative strategies and cutting-edge technologies to further refine their performance management system. They embraced experimentation and welcomed failure as an opportunity for growth, knowing that true excellence is born from relentless iteration.

As weeks turned into months and months into years, Emma and her team remained steadfast in their pursuit of excellence. They celebrated their successes but never grew complacent, always striving to push the boundaries of what was possible.

And in the end, their unwavering commitment to continuous improvement paid off. The organization flourished, its performance management system a beacon of innovation and effectiveness in the corporate landscape.

As Emma looked upon the fruits of their labor, she couldn't help but feel a swell of pride. The journey had been long and arduous, but the destination— a culture of excellence and continuous improvement— made every trial and tribulation worthwhile.

As Emma and her team embarked on their quest for continuous improvement, they knew that gathering feedback from employees and managers was paramount. They understood that the perspectives of those on the front lines were invaluable in shaping the evolution of their performance management system.

With this in mind, Emma devised a plan to collect feedback through a series of structured surveys, focus groups, and one-on-one interviews. She ensured that every voice within the organization had the opportunity to be heard, from entry-level employees to C-suite executives.

The process was not without its challenges. Some employees were hesitant to speak up, fearing reprisal or skepticism about the sincerity of the initiative. Others were eager to share their thoughts, relishing the chance to contribute to the organization's growth.

Emma and her team listened attentively to each voice, taking note of both praise and criticism. They analyzed trends and patterns, seeking to understand the underlying causes of dissatisfaction and identify opportunities for improvement.

"We cannot afford to ignore the feedback," Emma reminded her team. "Every comment, every suggestion— they are all pieces of the puzzle that will help us shape a better future for our organization."

Armed with a wealth of insights from their feedback collection efforts, Emma and her team set to work on implementing changes to their performance management system. They introduced new processes, revised existing policies, and launched targeted training programs to address areas of concern and capitalize on areas of strength.

The transformation was gradual but profound. Employees began to notice the changes, feeling empowered by the knowledge that their voices had been heard and their opinions valued. Morale soared, and a newfound sense of camaraderie permeated the organization as employees and managers alike rallied behind the shared goal of continuous improvement.

As the dust settled and the organization settled into its new normal, Emma couldn't help but feel a sense of pride. The journey had been long and challenging, but the destination— a culture of excellence and collaboration— made every step of the way worthwhile.

With the newly implemented performance management system in place, Emma understood that their work was far from over. Monitoring the effectiveness of the processes was essential to ensure ongoing success and identify areas for further improvement.

Gathering her team, Emma outlined a plan to systematically evaluate the performance management processes. They would track key metrics such as employee engagement scores, turnover rates, productivity levels, and performance appraisal completion rates.

As the weeks passed, Emma and her team meticulously analyzed the data, searching for trends and anomalies that could offer insights into the system's effectiveness. They poured over spreadsheets and reports, discussing their findings late into the night.

At times, the process was arduous, with seemingly contradictory data points causing frustration and confusion. But Emma remained steadfast, reminding her team that understanding the nuances of performance management required patience and persistence.

Finally, after weeks of analysis, patterns began to emerge. Employee engagement scores showed a steady increase, while turnover rates decreased significantly. Productivity levels were at an all-time high, and performance appraisal completion rates exceeded expectations.

"We've made significant progress," Emma declared, a sense of satisfaction evident in her voice. "But there's still work to be done. We must remain vigilant and continue to refine our processes to ensure that we're meeting the needs of our employees and the organization as a whole."

With renewed determination, Emma and her team set to work on implementing changes based on their findings. They fine-tuned their performance management processes, leveraging their newfound insights to drive further improvement and foster a culture of excellence within the organization.

With the initial success of the new performance management system, Emma knew that continuous improvement was essential to maintain momentum and achieve long-term success. She gathered her team once more, ready to make the necessary adjustments and refinements.

"Let's review the feedback we've received from employees and managers," Emma said, her voice filled with determination. "We need to identify areas where the system can be improved to better meet the needs of our diverse workforce."

Together, they poured over the feedback, noting recurring themes and suggestions for improvement. Some employees expressed a desire for more frequent feedback sessions, while others requested additional training on goal-setting and performance expectations.

Armed with this valuable insight, Emma and her team set to work, implementing changes to address the feedback received. They developed new training modules focused on goal alignment and performance coaching, equipping managers with the tools they needed to support their teams effectively.

In addition, they revamped the performance appraisal process, streamlining it to make it more user-friendly and aligned with the organization's goals. Emma ensured that the system remained flexible enough to adapt to the ever-changing needs of the workforce.

As the adjustments were implemented, Emma closely monitored their impact, tracking key metrics to gauge their effectiveness. Employee feedback remained positive, with many expressing appreciation for the organization's commitment to continuous improvement.

"We're making real progress," Emma remarked, a sense of pride evident in her voice. "But our work is far from over. We must remain vigilant and continue to listen to our employees, making adjustments and refinements as needed to ensure that our performance management system continues to evolve and meet the needs of our organization."

With renewed determination, Emma and her team pressed forward, confident in their ability to build a culture of excellence where every employee could thrive and succeed.

13

Chapter Thirteen: Case Studies in Effective Performance Management

In the mid st of the corporate whirlwind, Emma found herself eager to showcase the real-world impact of their revitalized performance management system. With the CEO's support, she decided to present a series of case studies highlighting the success stories of teams and individuals who had thrived under the new framework.

As the boardroom filled with eager faces, Emma took center stage, her confidence radiating as she prepared to share their triumphs.

"Let me introduce you to our first case study," Emma began, her voice steady and assured. "Meet Sarah, a project manager in our IT department."

With a click of the remote, the screen came to life, displaying images of Sarah and her team hard at work. Emma recounted how Sarah had embraced the new performance management system, leveraging its tools to set clear goals, provide regular feedback, and recognize her team's achievements.

"Under Sarah's leadership, the IT department saw a 20%

increase in productivity and a significant decrease in project turnaround time," Emma explained, pride evident in her voice. "Her team members reported higher job satisfaction and a renewed sense of purpose."

Next, Emma shifted focus to another case study, this time highlighting a sales team that had struggled under the old performance management system. With the implementation of targeted training and coaching sessions, coupled with a revamped incentive structure, the team had surpassed their targets and achieved record-breaking sales figures.

"As you can see, our new performance management system isn't just a theory," Emma proclaimed, her passion for their accomplishments shining through. "It's a proven framework that empowers our employees to excel, driving success at every level of the organization."

The boardroom buzzed with excitement as Emma concluded her presentation, the success stories serving as a beacon of hope for the future of their company. With each case study, Emma reinforced the belief that effective performance management was not just a strategy—it was the cornerstone of a culture of excellence and innovation.

As Emma delved deeper into her research, she uncovered real-world examples of organizations that had successfully implemented innovative performance management systems, each serving as a beacon of inspiration for her own transformational journey.

One such organization was Google, renowned for its pioneering approach to performance management. Emma marveled at Google's commitment to transparency, as evidenced by its practice of sharing performance data openly with employees. She marveled at how this approach fostered a culture of accountability and continuous improvement, empowering employees to take ownership of their performance and development.

Another standout example was Salesforce, where Emma found inspiration in the company's emphasis on regular feedback and coaching. She was impressed by Salesforce's use of technology to facilitate ongoing conversations between managers and employees, ensuring that feedback was timely, actionable, and tailored to individual needs. This focus on coaching and development resonated deeply with Emma, reinforcing her belief in the transformative power of continuous feedback.

As Emma studied these and other organizations, she gleaned valuable insights and best practices that she could apply to her own company's performance management overhaul. From Google's transparency to Salesforce's focus on coaching, each example served as a testament to the endless possibilities of effective performance management.

Armed with this newfound knowledge, Emma felt invigorated and inspired to continue her quest to build a culture of excellence within her organization. With each real-world example fueling her determination, she was more convinced than ever that success was within reach.

Emma's journey into the world of effective performance management led her to uncover invaluable lessons and best practices from real organizations that had successfully navigated similar challenges. Among these exemplars were companies like General Electric (GE) and Netflix, each offering unique insights into the art of cultivating a culture of excellence.

Drawing inspiration from GE, Emma learned about the power of differentiation in performance evaluation. She marveled at GE's rigorous performance ranking system, which encouraged healthy competition among employees and drove a relentless pursuit of excellence. Emma admired how GE's commitment to identifying and nurturing top talent had propelled the company to unparalleled success, inspiring her to explore new ways of recognizing and rewarding high performers within her own organization.

Similarly, Emma found herself captivated by Netflix's radical approach to performance management. She was intrigued by Netflix's emphasis on freedom and responsibility, which encouraged employees to take ownership of their work and pursue bold ideas without fear of failure. Emma admired how Netflix's culture of trust and autonomy had fueled innovation and creativity, prompting her to rethink traditional notions of performance evaluation and embrace a more agile and flexible approach.

As Emma reflected on the lessons learned from GE and Netflix, she realized that there was no one-size-fits-all solution to effective performance management. Instead, success lay in understanding the unique needs and dynamics of her own organization and tailoring her approach accordingly. Armed with this newfound wisdom, Emma felt empowered to continue her quest to build a culture of excellence within her company, confident that she was on the right path to unlocking its full potential.

As Emma delved deeper into the case studies of successful performance management systems, she found herself inspired by the innovative approaches adopted by companies like General Electric and Netflix. With each story, she gleaned valuable insights and lessons that she was eager to apply to her own organization.

Armed with newfound inspiration, Emma returned to her desk, ready to tackle the task of transforming her company's performance management framework. Drawing from GE's emphasis on differentiation, she began exploring ways to introduce a more rigorous ranking system that would incentivize high performance and foster healthy competition among employees.

At the same time, Emma reflected on Netflix's culture of freedom and responsibility, recognizing the importance of empowering employees to take ownership of their work and pursue innovative ideas. She vowed to instill a sense of trust and autonomy within her own organization, empowering employees to unleash their full potential and drive meaningful change.

With these insights in mind, Emma set out to refine her performance management system, incorporating elements of differentiation and autonomy to create a dynamic and employee-centric framework. She knew that the journey ahead would be challenging, but she was fueled by a newfound sense of purpose and determination to build a culture of excellence within her organization.

As Emma took the first steps towards implementing these changes, she felt a surge of excitement and anticipation. She knew that the road ahead would be filled with obstacles and challenges, but she was confident that with the right strategies and mindset, her organization could unlock its full potential and thrive in an environment of excellence and innovation.

14

Chapter Fourteen: Future Trends in Performance Management

As Emma's organization basked in the glow of its newfound success, she couldn't help but wonder about the future of performance management. She knew that in today's rapidly evolving business landscape, staying ahead of the curve was essential to maintaining a competitive edge.

Armed with a curious mind and a thirst for innovation, Emma delved into the latest research and industry insights, eager to uncover the future trends that would shape the world of performance management.

One trend that caught Emma's attention was the rise of artificial intelligence and data analytics in performance management. With advancements in technology, organizations were increasingly leveraging AI-powered tools to analyze vast amounts of data and gain actionable insights into employee performance. Emma saw this as an opportunity to enhance the accuracy and efficiency of performance evaluations, providing managers with real-time feedback and actionable recommendations to support decision-making.

CHAPTER FOURTEEN: FUTURE TRENDS IN PERFORMANCE MANAGEMENT

Another trend that piqued Emma's interest was the shift towards continuous feedback and coaching. Gone were the days of annual performance reviews; instead, organizations were embracing a more agile approach to performance management, with regular check-ins and ongoing conversations between managers and employees. Emma recognized the importance of fostering a culture of feedback and transparency within her own organization, empowering employees to take ownership of their development and growth.

As Emma delved deeper into the future of performance management, she couldn't help but feel a sense of excitement and optimism. She saw endless possibilities for innovation and improvement, and she was determined to lead her organization into the future with confidence and vision.

With each new trend she uncovered, Emma felt a renewed sense of purpose and determination. She knew that the journey ahead would be challenging, but she was fueled by a passion for excellence and a commitment to building a culture of continuous improvement within her organization.

As Emma looked towards the horizon, she saw a future filled with endless opportunities and possibilities. And with the right strategies and mindset, she knew that her organization could not only adapt to change but thrive in an ever-evolving business landscape.

The Performance Paradigm was not just a story of transformation; it was a testament to the power of innovation, resilience, and leadership in shaping the future of performance management. And as Emma continued on her journey, she knew that the best was yet to come.

As Emma delved deeper into the future of performance management, she couldn't ignore the profound impact that emerging technologies were having on the landscape of HR practices. With each passing day, new innovations were reshaping the way organizations approached performance evaluation and employee development.

One such technology that captured Emma's attention was artificial intelligence (AI). With its ability to process vast amounts of data and identify patterns, AI held the potential to revolutionize performance management. Emma envisioned AI-powered algorithms analyzing employee performance metrics in real-time, identifying areas for improvement, and even predicting future performance trends.

But AI was just the tip of the iceberg. Emma also explored the potential of wearable devices and biometric sensors in performance management. Imagine, she thought, employees wearing smartwatches or other wearable gadgets that tracked their physical activity, stress levels, and even mood throughout the workday. Such data could provide valuable insights into employee well-being and productivity, allowing organizations to tailor their performance management strategies accordingly.

As Emma envisioned the future of performance management, she couldn't help but feel a sense of excitement and possibility. The possibilities seemed endless, and she was determined to harness the power of these emerging technologies to drive her organization forward.

With each new advancement, Emma saw an opportunity to enhance the employee experience, foster a culture of continuous improvement, and ultimately, unlock the full potential of her organization. And as she looked towards the horizon, she knew that the future of performance management was brighter than ever before.

The Performance Paradigm was not just a story of trans-

CHAPTER FOURTEEN: FUTURE TRENDS IN PERFORMANCE MANAGEMENT

formation; it was a glimpse into the future of work, where innovation and technology were driving organizations towards new heights of success. And as Emma continued on her journey, she was ready to embrace the challenges and opportunities that lay ahead.

As Emma explored the future of performance management, she couldn't ignore the profound impact that shifts in organizational culture and leadership styles were having on the way companies approached performance evaluation and employee development.

In the past, traditional hierarchical structures dominated the corporate landscape, with top-down leadership styles dictating the direction of organizations. However, Emma noticed a seismic shift occurring—a move towards more agile, collaborative, and employee-centric cultures.

Leaders were no longer seen as distant figures issuing commands from on high; instead, they were expected to be coaches, mentors, and facilitators of growth. Emma envisioned a future where leaders embraced transparency, vulnerability, and empathy, fostering environments where employees felt valued, supported, and empowered to reach their full potential.

But changing organizational culture was no easy feat. Emma knew that it required strong leadership, open communication, and a willingness to challenge the status quo. Yet, she also recognized the immense rewards that awaited organizations brave enough to embrace this cultural shift.

As she pondered the future of leadership, Emma couldn't help but feel a sense of optimism. She saw leaders emerging who were not only visionary but also empathetic and inclusive. These leaders understood that the key to unlocking organizational success lay in unleashing the potential of every individual within the company.

With this newfound understanding, Emma felt more determined than ever to drive change within her organization. She knew that by championing a culture of collaboration, transparency, and empowerment, she could lay the foundation for a future where performance management was not just a process but a philosophy—a philosophy rooted in the belief that every employee had the power to make a difference.

And as Emma looked towards the horizon, she knew that the future of performance management was not just about embracing new technologies or methodologies; it was about embracing a new way of thinking—a way of thinking that put people at the center of everything. And with that realization, Emma felt a renewed sense of purpose, ready to lead her organization into a future where excellence was not just a goal but a way of life.

As Emma pondered the future of performance management, she couldn't help but speculate on the potential directions that practices in this field might take. Drawing on her experience and insights gained from her journey, she envisioned several key predictions for the future.

Firstly, Emma predicted a continued shift towards more agile and flexible performance management practices. Gone were the days of rigid annual performance reviews; instead, organizations would embrace continuous feedback loops and real-time performance monitoring. Emma foresaw a future where employees received feedback on their performance regularly, allowing for quicker course corrections and more meaningful development opportunities.

Secondly, Emma anticipated a greater emphasis on data-driven decision-making in performance management. With advancements in technology, organizations would have access to vast amounts of data about employee performance, engagement, and productivity. By leveraging analytics and artificial intelligence, Emma envisioned a future where organizations could make more informed decisions about talent management, succession planning, and resource allocation.

Additionally, Emma predicted an increased focus on holistic performance management approaches. Rather than solely evaluating individual performance in isolation, organizations would take a more holistic view, considering factors such as team dynamics, organizational culture, and employee well-being. Emma believed that this shift would lead to more comprehensive and equitable performance evaluations, ultimately driving better outcomes for both employees and organizations.

Finally, Emma foresaw a future where performance management became more personalized and tailored to individual needs. With the rise of customization and personalization in other areas of life, Emma believed that employees would come to expect performance management processes that were tailored to their unique strengths, preferences, and career aspirations. This would require organizations to adopt more flexible and adaptable performance management frameworks that could accommodate diverse needs and preferences.

As Emma reflected on these predictions, she felt a sense of excitement and optimism about the future of performance management. While the road ahead might be filled with challenges and uncertainties, Emma was confident that by embracing innovation, flexibility, and a people-centric approach, organizations could create a future where performance management truly optimized organizational success and employee performance.

15

Chapter Fifteen: Conclusion and Implementation Strategies

As Emma stood at the threshold of a new era for the organization's performance management, she reflected on the transformative journey she had undertaken. From the initial challenges and resistance to the remarkable successes and achievements, Emma had navigated through the complexities with determination and resilience. Now, as she prepared to conclude her mission, she outlined the key implementation strategies to ensure the sustained success of the new performance management paradigm.

First and foremost, Emma emphasized the importance of ongoing communication and education. Change was never easy, and it required constant communication and education to ensure buy-in and alignment across the organization. Emma vowed to continue educating leaders and employees about the principles and benefits of the new performance management system, fostering a shared understanding and commitment to its success.

Next, Emma highlighted the need for continuous evaluation

and refinement. The journey towards excellence was never truly over, and Emma stressed the importance of monitoring the effectiveness of the new performance management system and making adjustments as needed. By collecting feedback, analyzing data, and soliciting input from stakeholders, Emma planned to continuously refine and improve the system to ensure it remained relevant and impactful.

Furthermore, Emma emphasized the importance of leadership accountability and role modeling. Leaders set the tone for organizational culture and performance, and Emma was committed to holding leaders accountable for championing the new performance management practices and leading by example. Through training, coaching, and recognition, Emma aimed to empower leaders to effectively implement and support the new system.

Lastly, Emma underscored the importance of celebrating successes and recognizing progress. Change was often accompanied by challenges and setbacks, but it was also important to acknowledge and celebrate the achievements along the way. Emma planned to celebrate milestones, recognize individuals and teams for their contributions, and showcase the tangible impact of the new performance management system on organizational success and employee performance.

As Emma concluded her reflections, she felt a sense of pride and satisfaction in the journey she had undertaken. The road ahead might still be filled with challenges and uncertainties, but Emma was confident that with the right strategies and mindset, the organization would continue to thrive in a culture of excellence and innovation, unlocking its full potential through effective performance management.

As Emma concluded her journey in redesigning the performance management framework, she gathered her team and the company's leadership to summarize the key takeaways from their transformative experience. Standing before them, she spoke with passion and conviction, distilling the essence of their collective journey into actionable insights.

"First and foremost," Emma began, her voice resonating with authority and warmth, "we've learned that effective performance management is not just about processes and metrics; it's about people. It's about recognizing the unique strengths and contributions of each individual and aligning their goals with the broader objectives of the organization."

She paused, allowing her words to sink in before continuing, "Secondly, we've seen firsthand the power of continuous feedback and recognition. By fostering a culture of feedback and recognition, we can empower our employees to reach their full potential and drive organizational success."

Emma's eyes sparkled with intensity as she emphasized her next point, "Thirdly, we must never underestimate the importance of leadership accountability. Leaders play a crucial role in shaping organizational culture and performance, and it's imperative that they lead by example, championing the values and practices of effective performance management."

She took a moment to survey the faces before her, noting the nods of agreement and the attentive expressions. Then, with a determined smile, she delivered her final point, "And lastly, we must embrace change as an opportunity for growth and innovation. Change may be daunting, but it's also the catalyst for progress. By embracing change with courage and creativity, we can unlock new possibilities and chart a course towards a future of excellence."

As Emma concluded her remarks, she felt a sense of satis-

CHAPTER FIFTEEN: CONCLUSION AND IMPLEMENTATION STRATEGIES

faction wash over her. The journey had been challenging, but it had also been incredibly rewarding. And as she looked out at the eager faces before her, she knew that they were ready to embark on the next chapter of their collective journey—a future filled with endless possibilities and untapped potential.

With the momentum of their successful transformation behind them, Emma knew that the journey was far from over. As she stood before her team and the company's leadership, she outlined a comprehensive action plan for implementing and improving performance management throughout the organization.

"Firstly," Emma began, her voice steady and resolute, "we must ensure that our performance management system is aligned with our organizational goals and values. This means establishing clear objectives and metrics that reflect our strategic priorities and vision for the future."

She paused, allowing her words to sink in before continuing, "Next, we must prioritize transparency and communication. We need to ensure that employees understand the purpose and process of performance management, and that they feel empowered to actively participate in their own development."

Emma's eyes sparkled with determination as she emphasized her next point, "Thirdly, we must leverage technology to streamline and enhance the performance management process. From automated feedback systems to data analytics tools, technology can play a crucial role in driving efficiency and effectiveness."

She took a moment to gauge the reactions of her audience before proceeding, "And finally, we must cultivate a culture of continuous learning and improvement. Performance management is not a one-time event; it's an ongoing journey of growth and development. By fostering a culture of continuous learning and improvement, we can ensure that our performance management system remains dynamic and responsive to the evolving needs of our organization."

As Emma concluded her remarks, she felt a sense of excitement and anticipation wash over her. The road ahead would undoubtedly be challenging, but she was confident that with the right strategies and mindset, they could continue to build upon their successes and unlock even greater potential for excellence and innovation within the organization.

As Emma concluded her presentation on the implementation strategies for performance management, she looked around the room, meeting the eyes of each member of the leadership team. With a deep breath, she began her final thoughts on the importance of continuous improvement and adaptation in performance management.

"Change is inevitable," Emma stated, her voice carrying a tone of conviction. "In today's fast-paced business environment, organizations must be agile and adaptable to thrive. This applies not only to our products and services but also to how we manage and develop our most valuable asset: our people."

She paused, allowing her words to resonate with her audience before continuing, "Continuous improvement is not just a buzzword; it's a mindset. It's about constantly seeking ways to enhance our processes, systems, and practices to better serve our employees and achieve our organizational goals."

Emma's gaze swept across the room, capturing the attention of every listener. "Performance management is not a static concept," she emphasized. "It's a dynamic and ever-evolving discipline that requires us to be open to new ideas, technologies, and approaches."

CHAPTER FIFTEEN: CONCLUSION AND IMPLEMENTATION STRATEGIES

"With each challenge we face and each success we achieve, we must remain committed to learning and growing," Emma declared, her voice brimming with passion. "By embracing a culture of continuous improvement and adaptation, we can ensure that our performance management practices remain relevant, effective, and aligned with the needs of our organization and its people."

As Emma concluded her final thoughts, she felt a sense of satisfaction knowing that she had laid the groundwork for a future where performance management was not just a process but a guiding philosophy—a paradigm shift that would propel the organization toward even greater heights of excellence and success.

About the Author

Goodson Mumba is a multifaceted individual known for his diverse expertise and prolific contributions across various fields. As an infopreneur, thought leader, and spiritual leader, he has inspired countless individuals through his insightful teachings and impactful writings. Mumba is also an accomplished author, with several notable works to his name, including "Understanding Corporate Worship," "The Years I Spent in a Week," "Management By Harmony," "The CEO's Diary," "Change to Change" and "Creative Thinking for results" His literary works span topics ranging from business management to personal development and spirituality, reflecting his broad range of interests and insights.

With a Master of Business Leadership (MBL) and a Bachelor of Arts in Theology (BTh), Mumba brings a unique blend of business acumen and spiritual wisdom to his work. His educational background is further enriched by a Group Diploma in Management Studies, providing him with a solid foundation in organizational dynamics and leadership principles. Additionally, Mumba holds diplomas in Education Psychology,

Leadership and Management Styles, Organizational Behaviour, Financial Accounting, Economic Growth and Development, and Project Management, showcasing his commitment to continuous learning and professional development.

Mumba's expertise extends beyond traditional academic disciplines, encompassing areas such as Neuro-Linguistic Programming (NLP) and Positive Psychology. His diverse skill set is complemented by a range of certifications, including Creative Problem Solving and Decision Making, Life Coaching Fundamentals and Techniques, Professional Life Coaching, and Performance Management System Design. These certifications reflect Mumba's dedication to equipping himself with the tools and knowledge necessary to empower others and drive positive change.

As an author, Mumba's writings reflect his deep understanding of human nature, organizational dynamics, and spiritual principles. His works offer practical insights, actionable strategies, and inspirational guidance for individuals seeking personal growth, professional success, and spiritual fulfillment. Mumba's holistic approach to life and leadership resonates with readers worldwide, making him a respected figure in both the business and spiritual communities.

Overall, Goodson Mumba's diverse background, extensive knowledge, and profound insights make him a sought-after speaker, mentor, and author. His commitment to excellence, lifelong learning, and service to others continues to inspire individuals to unlock their full potential and lead lives of purpose and significance.

Goodson Mumba is renowned for initiating the concept of Management by Harmony, revolutionizing traditional management practices with a focus on balanced and holistic approaches. He has authored two influential books on this subject: "Introduction to Management by Harmony" and its sequel, "Management by Harmony."

Mumba's work has significantly impacted the field, offering innovative strategies for fostering organizational harmony and efficiency. His contributions continue to shape contemporary management theories and practices.

www.ingramcontent.com/pod-product-compliance
Lightning Source LLC
Chambersburg PA
CBHW071835210526
45479CB00001B/151